BRITNEY Spears

Unstoppable!

The Unofficial Book of the Britney Experience

TRIUMPH ENTERTAINMENT
Division of Triumph Books

Contents

John Delevan/Executive Editor
Elliott From/Creative Director
Erin Brereton/Senior Editor
Laurel Smoke/Assistant Editor
Karin Kaltofen/Managing Art Director
Stacy Lipner/Photo Editor
Natalie Cooper/Graphic Designer

Photos: Wildshots LLC, Corbis Outline, Shooting Star, Kevin Mazur Photography, Retna Ltd., Sean McCloskey Sports Imagery, Seth Poppel Yearbook Archives, Dennis Jourdan Photography, Globe, Stacey Hewey, John Delevan, Bill Apter, Dale Woltman

UP FRONT WITH BRITNEY

From rumors to realities, clothing to career, Miss Spears comes clean

By Nicole Neville

You're one of the busiest people in music – your life must be crazy! How do you take your mind off everything?
I just do normal things like call my mom and my girlfriends, or I go to the movies or the beach. I usually have one day off per week when I can sleep late and just hang out.

When you go home, do your old friends ever say they think you've changed since you've become famous?
No, not at all. We never feel weird; we're like sisters. If they kissed my butt, I would kick their butts!

Who are your closest friends?
I'm good friends with my dancers and my cousins from home; I've been friends with them my whole life. My mom's sister's daughter, Laura Lynne, we're very close. She's my age and our mannerisms are exactly alike.

Do you have new friends now that you're a star?
It's really hard to find friends. I am fortunate that the people who travel with me, especially my dancers, are really good friends. It works out very well.

What was your life like before you made it big?
Well, I was performing at malls. There was a little fashion show before I performed, and it was before my first single ("...Baby One More Time") came out, so no one really knew who I was. But it was cool because I had two dancers with me and we put on a cute little show. Everyone was really into it, and that made me feel good.

LEFT TO RIGHT: JON RAGEL/OUTLINE; TARA CANOVA/RETNA

"My mom is so positive about life. She's not negative; she always looks on the bright side of everything."

Britney with mom Lynne at the 1999 Teen Choice Awards

How did you first get into singing and dancing?
When I was little, we had a gym right beside our house, and there was this lady who taught dance there. I started dancing when I was really young. Then I started gymnastics. I'd sing to the radio all the time, and I was in the church choir, and I just realized that I loved to sing. I started doing competitions and I continued dancing, so it all kind of came together.

You starred on "The New Mickey Mouse Club" along with JC Chasez and Justin Timberlake of *NSYNC, not to mention Christina Aguilera. Everyone's really successful now. Did you keep in touch over the years?
I was going to be in a girl's group called Innosense before I got signed a solo deal with Jive Records. Justin's mom (who manages Innosense) and my mom kept in touch, and Lynn, Justin's mom, told me about it. But I signed with Jive instead, so I didn't join the group.

Do you have a role model?
Definitely my mom because she is so positive about life. She's not negative; she always looks on the bright side of everything. I really admire that. I would also love to meet Oprah Winfrey or Whitney Houston.

Is Madonna one of your heroes?
I just admire how she is able to reinvent herself and keep the public interested in her music.

We heard that Barbra Streisand is also a major influence.
Yeah. When I was younger, I listened to her music a lot, and I still listen to her periodically. I would love to meet her.

What do you think about little girls who want to be like you?
I think it is very flattering. I have a little sister, and it is really special to have her look up to me that way. She goes in my room and plays my music. She's so sweet. And she is so outspoken. She' totally different from what I was lik when I was little. I was a very quiet child

So do you think of yourself as a role model for other girls?
I think it's inevitable. When you're o

Britney belts out one of her hits at the annual "Wango Tango" concert at Dodger Stadium in Los Angeles.

TV all the time and in magazines, you can't help but be one.

Is that a role you're willing to take on?
Yeah, definitely. It's really flattering that so many kids listen to my music. It's really cool!

So what's next besides singing? Producing? Acting?
I would love to act AND write songs. When I get time, I would love to act more.

Do you have any offers?
Oh yeah. I have some offers to be in some movies, and some of them are kind of, you know, so-so. Some scripts, though, have been really good, and I say, "I want to do that." It's just (a matter of) finding the time to fit filming a movie into my schedule.

You've already appeared on "Sabrina, the Teenage Witch," and you'll be in the upcoming movie "Jack of All Trades." Will there be more Britney on the big screen?
All I can say is I would definitely like to keep acting.

What's the deal with your movie role in "Jack of All Trades"?
I play a flight attendant. It's a small role.

You have said that you eventually want to go to college. Is that still true?
It is definitely something I want to do if I have time. To have that education would be wonderful. But what I really want to do with my life is to sing. So why should I go to college to learn to be, say, a lawyer, when I'm happy doing what I'm doing now?

Do you consider yourself to be a spiritual person?
I try to go to church whenever I can. I also have a prayer book that I write in every night. When I'm on the road I get so tired, and I used to find myself falling asleep when I'd say my prayers at night. So now I write my prayers down before I go to bed.

Fashion, Fun and Food

What kinds of clothes do you like to wear?
When I'm traveling, I'm typically tired, so that usually means I'm in sweats. When I go out to eat or go to parties, I usually wear (clothes from) bebe. My favorite store in the world is Abercrombie & Fitch. It's the best store because its clothes are all about comfort; it's cool and I love it.

Has fame changed the way you dress?
It hasn't really changed my style at all. I've always been a big sweats person, and I like putting my hair in a ponytail.

What do you have way too many of?
Probably sunglasses. Wherever I go – gas stations, Sunglass Hut – I'm always buying new shades!

How many pairs do you have?
I travel with about six pairs, but I have at least three dozen.

If you could change something about your appearance, what would it be?
I wish my hair was thicker, and I wish my feet were prettier. I don't like my feet. My toes – they're really ugly. I also wish my ears were smaller, and my nose could be smaller, too. I could go on and on (laughing)!

Have your eating habits changed since you became famous?
When I'm on the road, I tend to eat bad things – I can't help it. Like when I'm overseas, I typically don't want to eat all that weird stuff. I just want McDonald's to fill up my stomach. I normally eat whatever I want, but I'm trying to be a little bit healthier. When I go home to Louisiana, my mom cooks for me, so that's when I have my best meals!

"I would love to act and write songs. When I get time, I would love to act more."

LEFT TO RIGHT: PAUL FENTON/SHOOTING STAR, JON RAGEL/OUTLINE, STEVE GRANITZ/RETNA

" I try to go to church whenever I can. I also have a prayer book that I write in every night."

Do you have any special rituals before you perform?
I always say a prayer. And I drink a lot of water.

What's something you heard about yourself that's completely false?
The rumors about the breast enlargements . . . those rumors are just not true.

Now that you have fame and fortune, what's been your biggest splurge?
A white convertible Mercedes SL 500. My grandmother could get picked up in this car it's so beautiful. (Britney also recently decided to have a bigger house built for her and her family in her hometown.)

Do you have a favorite homemade meal?
Probably my mom's baked chicken. It tastes so good. And she makes the crust really crunchy.

What can't you resist?
Cookie-dough ice cream! I like fast food, too, like a chicken sandwich with cheese from Burger King. I just crave that sometimes! And greasy french fries and a Coke. They are so bad for you, but they taste so good!

What are your fave snacks?
I'm a cereal girl – I like Apple Jacks. And macaroni and cheese at night.

Do you cook?
Nope.

Do you clean up?
Yeah, I clean up. I wash the dishes, I vacuum. I clean, make my bed. I do everything!

You're from a super- small town – Kentwood, La. What's that like?
Kentwood has only 1,200 people. But the mall is 30 minutes away, and it's in a bigger city. And it's really cool, though, because where I'm from, you'd think more people would know me — and they do, but they totally respect that I'm trying to lead a somewhat normal life.

If you go out to the mall with your friends, can you just shop or do you get recognized?
It's weird when I go to really big malls because people will notice me. I've been to a couple of malls where it was a bit overwhelming. But my hometown mall is the coolest. No one says anything to me.

Wild & Crazy

Do you believe in aliens?
No.

Do you read your horoscope?
Oh yeah, all the time.

What's your sign?
I'm a Sagittarius.

What does that mean about you?
I travel a lot, which is true. And it's a fire sign, so I have a lot of energy.

Growing up, did you ever wish your name was something else?
Madison. I love the name Madison.

If you could be invisible for a day, whom would you spy on?
My ex-boyfriend…just to see…

If you could sing a duet with anyone, whom would it be?
Ricky Martin. He's very expressive – and he's cute!

What TV shows do you watch?
"Felicity" and "Dawson's Creek."

What kind of music do you like?
Brandy, Lauryn Hill, Whitney Houston, TLC…I like old music, too, like Rick Springfield, John Mellencamp – stuff like that.

Do you have a favorite movie?
"Steel Magnolias." And "Beaches." Those movies make me cry and cry!

Did you go to your prom?
My ex-boyfriend was a senior, so I went to his prom (when I was a freshman). So I've experienced that. The best part of going to the prom is getting ready. You know how the night goes — you go to the dance for 15 minutes and leave, and all you do afterwards is get trashed. I didn't do that, though.

Finish this sentence: One day see myself...
Eventually there will come a time when I want to settle down and have kid and be completely normal. But that's a long way away, so we'll just have to see

What one message do you have for your fans?
I'm just being myself, and hopefull that comes across in my music and peopl dig that. ♥

FiftyBritn

Think you know all there is to know about Miss Spears? See how many of these Fun Facts you already knew!

By Amy Helmes

yFunFacts

TIMOTHY WHITE/OUTLINE

1. RAGIN' CAJUN

Britney was a bayou baby. Her hometown is Kentwood, La. (population: 1,200), about an hour's drive north of New Orleans.

2. PUPPY LOVE

For Christmas, Britney's mom gave her a Yorkie teacup puppy named Mitzi. After some extensive potty training, Mitzi can now accompany Britney on tour.

3. RAISING THE ROOF

She and her mother, Lynne, are designing an English Tudor-style dream house.

4. ROAD WARRIOR

Britney loves riding four-wheelers and go-carts with her sister, Jamie Lynn.

5. KNEE-SLAPPERS

Besides keeping her safe, Britney's bodyguards provide an extra service — making her laugh.

6. COLLECT CALL

When she's on tour, Britney calls her mom nearly every night.

7. ROOM WITH A VIEW ... OF THE FREEWAY!

Brit's room on her tour bus is painted lilac and decorated with gifts from fans.

8. THE WEDDING SINGER

Before she made it big, Britney performed at relatives' weddings.

9. FAN MAIL

Candles and dolls are a few of the favorite gifts Britney has received from fans.

10. GLASS SLIPPERS

Britney collects tiny porcelain shoes.

11. NICE NIGHT OUT

The pop star's idea of a perfect date is a good movie and a nice meal at a restaurant.

12. GLOBE-TROTTING

Britney's favorite vacation spots are jolly old England and the beautiful Bahamas.

13. COLLEGE PREP

Britney says she'd eventually love to go to college and study entertainment law.

14. SUN GODDESS

A favorite pastime is soaking up rays to perfect her tan. She'll even go to a tanning salon on cold or cloudy days.

15. GRAB THE KLEENEX!

Her favorite flicks: "Steel Magnolias" and "My Best Friend's Wedding."

16. HOT WHEELS

Britney recently purchased a convertible Jaguar but she can't find time to drive it!

17. PAGE TURNER

Trashy romance novels are Britney's guilty pleasure. Her favorite book is Danielle Steele's "Dangerous."

18. MOBILE MASTERPIECE

Britney thinks the cell phone is one of society's greatest inventions. She's always using hers to catch up with friends from home. She loves e-mail, too.

19. MAKING THE GRADE

Although she's a teen queen, Britney still has schoolwork. Her least favorite subjects? Geometry and Spanish.

20. MAGIC KINGDOM

As a former Mouseketeer, Britney knows her way around Walt Disney World. Her favorite attractions at the enormous theme park are Space Mountain and Rockin' Rollercoaster.

21. HOOP DREAMS

Britney has always felt at home on a basketball court, and she's a big fan of the Chicago Bulls.

22. BORN TO HAND JIVE

Britney is "hopelessly devoted" to the "Grease" movie soundtrack.

23. BIGGEST SLIP-UP

Even Britney has had a few embarrassing moments. Once, at an *NSYNC concert, she slipped on a cupcake and fell.

24. BEAUTY BUZZ

Her favorite brand of makeup is MAC.

25. THE NAME GAME

If Britney could choose a different name, she'd pick Madison or Alana.

26. QUIET RIOT

She may shine on stage, but in real life, Britney describes herself as quiet and shy.

27. SISTER ACT

Britney's most memorable moment was the birth of her little sister, Jamie Lynn.

28. MEAL TICKET

Chicken and dumplings and cookie dough ice cream are some of Britney's favorite foods.

29. DUELING DIVAS

Someday Britney would love to sing a duet with Madonna.

30. CHURCH LADY

Apparently, Britney is so religious that she's a little upset about having to miss church services while she's touring.

31. TWIST OF FATE

The man who wrote "...Baby One More Time" originally intended it to be sung by TLC, but he later changed his mind and gave it to Britney instead.

32. COOL THREADS

Although Britney has a personal stylist for most of her public appearances, some of her favorite designers include Betsey Johnson, bebe and Giorgio Armani.

33. I THEE WED?

Britney says she doesn't think she'll get married until she's at least 26 years old.

34. THIS LITTLE PIGGY...

Though Britney's feet are great for dancing, she likes that body part least.

35. CAFFEINE CONFUSION

Two of Britney's favorite drinks are Sprite and cappuccino.

36. CREATIVE LICENSE

The schoolgirl theme in the video for the No. 1 single "...Baby One More Time" was Britney's idea. It was reportedly the most requested video ever on MTV's "Total Request Live."

37. KISS AND TELL

Rumor has it Britney's first kiss was with *NSYNC's Justin Timberlake. They "went out" briefly while starring together on "The New Mickey Mouse Club."

38. SCARY MOMENT

A crazed fan once climbed into Britney's parents' bedroom window. Creepy!

39. OFF HER CHEST

Contrary to rumors, Britney swears that she has never gotten breast implants. She says anyone who believes that gossip is an "ignorant goofball."

40. SHATTERING RECORDS

Britney was the first female artist to simultaneously have the No. 1 pop single and No. 1 album (according to Billboard) in the United States.

41. TONGUE-TIED

Although Britney is a superstar in her own right, she says she gets nervous meeting other celebrities.

42. MAMA'S GIRL

Teenage girls may butt heads with their mothers, but Britney's is her best friend. She showed her gratitude by giving mom a new car and a diamond bracelet.

43. GAL PALS

Britney looks for complete honesty in a friend, even if she doesn't want to hear it. One good friend is Danielle Fishel, star of ABC's "Boy Meets World."

44. BREAK A LEG

Last year, Britney underwent knee surgery after she tore some cartilage during dance practice.

45. DID YOU KNOW?

The video for "...Baby One More Time" was shot at the same high school where the movie "Grease" was filmed.

46. METAL MOUTH

Her pearly whites may look perfect now, but it took a little work. Britney wore braces in high school.

47. BALANCING ACT

Britney was once enrolled in a gymnastics camp with legendary Olympic gymnastics coach Bela Karolyi. She kept a balance beam in her parents' living room.

48. COUCH POTATO

Britney's favorite TV shows are WB hits "Felicity" and "Dawson's Creek."

49. WHO'S THAT GIRL?

The woman who plays the teacher in the "...Baby One More Time" video is a close family friend who acts as Britney's guardian on the road.

50. CELEBRITY CRUSH

Like most teenage girls, Britney thinks Ben Affleck is a big-time hottie. (Unlike most girls, though, she got to have lunch with Ben!) She also digs Tom Cruise, Mel Gibson and Brad Pitt. ♥

LEFT TO RIGHT: MAX SMITH/RETNA; PAUL FENTON/SHOOTING STAR

Lookin' Go

Take a peek inside Britney's beauty bag and learn how to steal her style

Whether she's on MTV's "TRL," dancing in her latest video or performing on tour or at an awards show, Britney Spears always looks absolutely fabulous from head to toe. The designer duds she shows up in may cost big bucks, but her fave beauty products are in everyone's price range. Check out the six indulgences Britney swears by.

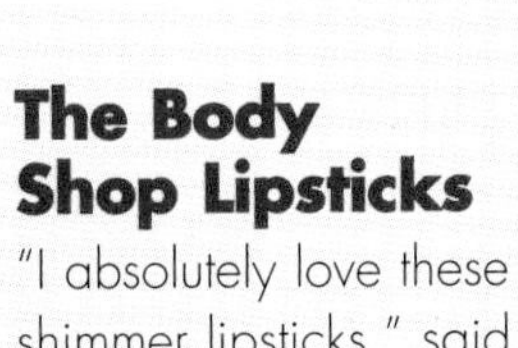

The Body Shop Lipsticks

"I absolutely love these shimmer lipsticks," said Britney. "The Body Shop has the best ones."

od

"I'll use a little Clinique toner after I wash my face to tighten up my pores. It makes my face feel clean."

PRODUCT PHOTOS BY DENNIS JOURDAN PHOTOGRAPHY; OPPOSITE PAGE, TOP TO BOTTOM: MARC BAPTISTE/OUTLINE, MATTHEW JORDAN SMITH/OUTLINE, JOHN BARRETT/GLOBE, NINA PROMMER/GLOBE; THIS PAGE: JON RAGEL/OUTLINE

Lookin' Good

Vanilla Lace perfume by Victoria's Secret
"I love vanilla!" Enough said.

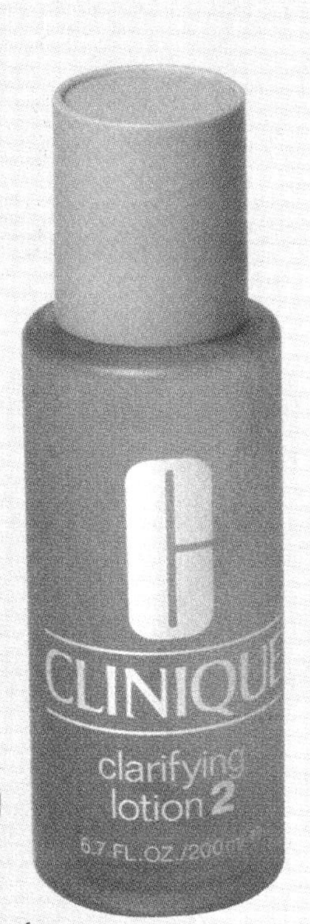

Clinique Clarifying Lotion 2
"I'll use a little Clinique toner after I wash my face to tighten up my pores. It makes my face feel clean."

Bath & Body Works Moisture-Rich Body Lotion in Vanilla Bean
"If there's one thing I really love, it's the lotions from Bath & Body Works. They're really, really thick."

Feel Perfecte Foundation by L'Oréal
"After I use the toner, I'll put this on. It makes your face look flawless. And it's made from the same company as Lancôme — it's just $15 cheaper."

The Body Shop Eyeshadows
"I love browns. I'll use a darker one on my lid and a lighter one on my browbone."

"If there's one thing I really love, it's the lotions from Bath & Body Works."

PRODUCT PHOTOS BY DENNIS JOURDAN PHOTOGRAPHY
THIS PAGE: JON RAGEL/OUTLINE

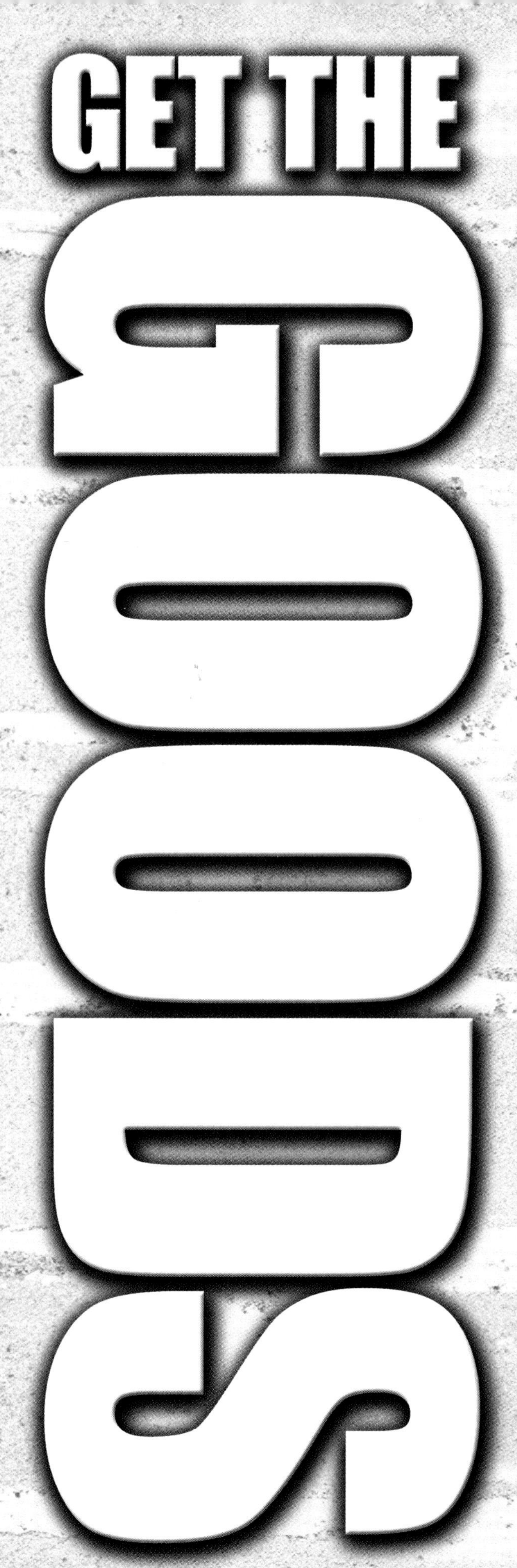

Be prepared to empty your piggy bank if you want to own all of Britney's CDs and other cool stuff

Even the most devoted Britney Spears fan would face a huge challenge trying to collect all of Britney's CDs and other Britney-related items. In just over two years in the international spotlight, Britney has released a flood of merchandise, from full-length compact discs (and hard-to-find CD singles) to Britney dolls, home videos, posters, books and bubble gum.

"Britney mania" is a worldwide phenomenon, and with Britney's third album hitting stores later this year, don't expect it to end anytime soon! How many of her CDs and other items do you own?

Britney Spears Discography

FULL-LENGTH ALBUMS

...Baby One More Time
Release Date: Jan. 12, 1999
Track Listing
01. ...Baby One More Time
02. (You Drive Me) Crazy
03. Sometimes
04. Soda Pop
05. Born To Make You Happy
06. From The Bottom Of My Broken Heart
07. I Will Be There
08. I Will Still Love You (featuring Don Philip)
09. Thinkin' About You
10. E-Mail My Heart
11. The Beat Goes On

Oops! ... I Did It Again
Release Date: May 16, 2000
1. Oops! ... I Did It Again
2. Stronger
3. Don't Go Knockin' On My Door
4. Satisfaction (I Can't Get No)
5. Don't Let Me Be The Last To Know
6. What U See (Is What U Get)
7. Lucky
8. One Kiss From You
9. Where Are You Now
10. Can't Make You Love Me
11. When Your Eyes Say It
12. Dear Diary

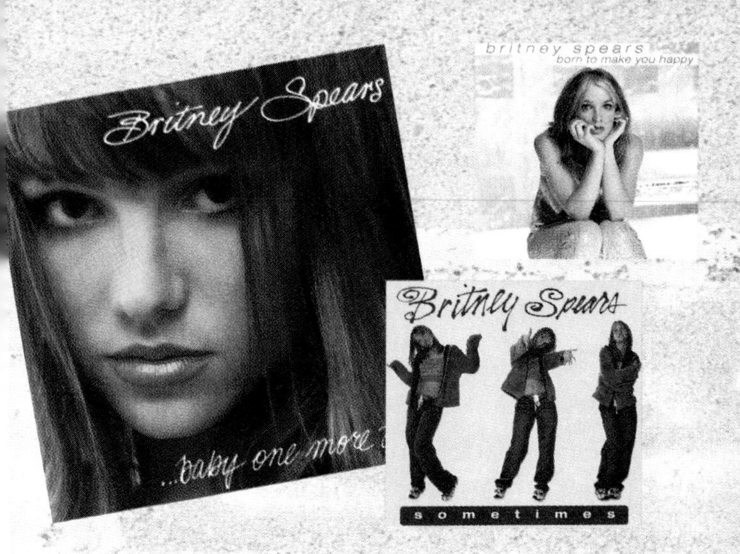

CD SINGLES

(in North America and/or Europe)
* **...Baby One More Time** (with dance remixes plus previously unreleased B-side "Autumn Goodbye")
* **Sometimes** (with dance remixes plus previously unreleased B-side "I'm So Curious")
* **Born To Make You Happy** (released only outside North America)
* **(You Drive Me) Crazy** (includes several remixes)
* **From The Bottom Of My Broken Heart** (radio edit plus additional remix of "Crazy")

Note: Several versions of many CD singles exist, with different "bonus tracks" depending on when and where the CD single was released.

HOME VIDEOS

If you're a big Brit fan, "Time Out With Britney Spears" (on VHS and DVD) is a must for your Britney collection. OK, the vid isn't going to win any Academy Awards for best documentary, but it's got plenty of stuff to keep you entertained for several viewings.

Britney starts the tape by giving a little background about her early days as a performer, when she was a budding gymnast instead of a singer! Eventually, of course, she went on to pursue a career in music, a career that got a huge lift from her role on Disney's "The New Mickey Mouse Club" in the mid-1990s.

Britney then takes you behind the scenes of the recording of her debut album in the spring of 1998 and for the filming of her first three music videos: "...Baby One More Time," "Sometimes" and "(You Drive Me) Crazy." While the backstage info is pretty interesting, perhaps the best part of this segment is the inclusion of all three music videos in their entirety. Since it's almost impossible to record a complete video off MTV these days (every vid on "TRL" is cut off way before it ends), you'll appreciate having Britney's videos in this collection.

Also featured are two performances from Britney's concert on The Disney Channel: "Born To Make You Happy" and "From The Bottom Of My Broken Heart."

One final bonus: Included with the video/DVD is a cassette sampler featuring new Jive Records artists such as Steps ("Tragedy") and Aaron Carter ("Girl You Shine"). The tunes are fun, so give 'em a listen.

BOOKS

Britney's new, official book, "Britney Spears' Heart to Heart," should be in stores by the time you read this. In the book, the American singing sensation and her mom talk about life, love, fame and following your dreams.

Britney makes success look simple. As Brit will tell you, though, success is hard work – you need talent, belief in yourself and someone else who believes in you. For Britney, that person has always been her mother, Lynne Spears, who is not just Britney's mom but also her best friend.

In "Britney Spears' Heart to Heart," Britney and Lynne share the inspiring story of how one little girl from Kentwood, La., turned into a music phenomenon. From the days of singing at talent shows and family gatherings to recording "...Baby One More Time" and performing with 'NSYNC, Britney and Lynne share intimate details about Britney's rise to stardom.

But this book is much more than just the story of Britney's life. In their own words, Lynne and Britney talk openly about the challenges facing all mothers and daughters. How do you encourage your child? How do you talk to your mom? How do you overcome obstacles? How do you talk about dating and relationships, dress codes, self-esteem and body image?

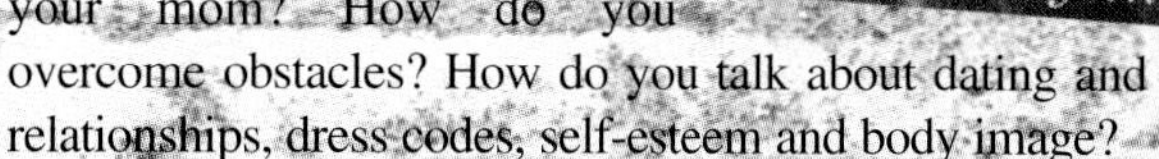

Featuring never-before-seen photos and dozens of behind-the-scenes stories about life at home, in the studio, and on the road, "Britney Spears' Heart to Heart" is not only a must-have for Britney fans, it's also an honest look at what it's like for girls to grow up in today's world.

THE BRITNEY DOLLS

Britney's three official dolls, which hit stores in time for the holidays, were a huge hit! Each doll came with separate outfits mirroring the clothes Britney wore in her first three music videos: "...Baby One More Time," "Sometimes" and "(You Drive Me) Crazy."

If you're an avid collector, buy all the dolls and keep them in their original boxes. They could be worth big money someday! ♥

MARC BAPTISTE/OUTLINE

FREAK
TIGI

Test your
B.I.Q.
Britney Intelligence Quotient!

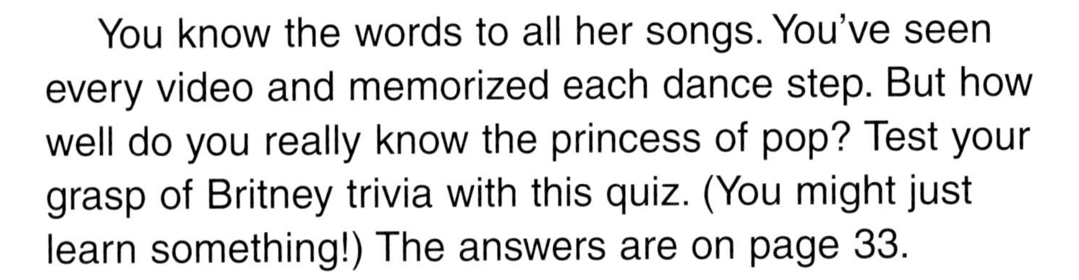

You know the words to all her songs. You've seen every video and memorized each dance step. But how well do you really know the princess of pop? Test your grasp of Britney trivia with this quiz. (You might just learn something!) The answers are on page 33.

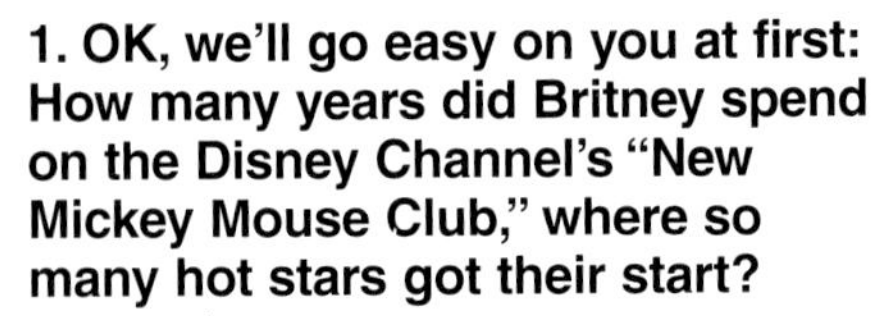

1. OK, we'll go easy on you at first: How many years did Britney spend on the Disney Channel's "New Mickey Mouse Club," where so many hot stars got their start?
  a. 1
  b. 2
  c. 3
  d. 4

2. While she was a Mouseketeer, Britney hung out with lots of teens who went on to have pretty impressive careers of their own. Which of these headline-grabbing names did not appear in the *MMC* credits with Britney's?
  a. JC Chasez
  b. Keri Russell
  c. Sarah Michelle Gellar
  d. Justin Timberlake

3. Every girl's got to splurge once in awhile. When Britney feels like kicking back in comfy sweats with a big bowl of ice cream, what flavor does she grab?
  a. strawberry
  b. mint chip
  c. chocolate
  d. cookie dough

4. Even though her super-busy life doesn't leave many free minutes for romance, Britney would definitely make time for:
  a. Brad Pitt
  b. James Van Der Beek
  c. Seth Green
  d. Ricky Martin

5. When she's relaxing with family or friends, Britney likes a little TV time. Which of these shows is not one of her must-sees?
  a. "Dawson's Creek"
  b. "Friends"
  c. "The Simpsons"
  d. "Felicity"

6. Britney was one motivated little girl! When she was just 10 years old, she did the theater thing and had a starring role in the off-Broadway show *Ruthless*. What was her character?
  a. a gang gal
  b. a kid who would do anything to be a star
  c. a grouchy cheerleader
  d. a girl who gets even with her best friend for stealing her guy

7. Ever since she was just a kid, this diva has loved music (and singing). You might say she's a natural in the biz. But that songstress urge had to start somewhere, like in the albums she listened to. What's her favorite song from way back when?
  a. "Control"
  b. "Material Girl"
  c. "Sweet Child o' Mine"
  d. "Purple Rain"

8. Britney's hometown of Kentwood, La., is a small place. (Some blocks in New York City have more residents than all of her town!) So traveling to foreign countries took a bit of getting used to for the young star. When Britney boarded her first flight to another country, where was she heading?
  a. Sweden
  b. Japan
  c. France
  d. Great Britain

9. As a major superstar, Britney is beyond popular. Tons of people know who she is, and sometimes that gets kind of weird. The perfect example: What did she find at her home during Christmas in 1998?

a. a package with an engagement ring from someone she'd never met
b. an obsessed male fan
c. a packet of letters from a fourth-grade class in Chicago
d. a huge teddy bear from a secret admirer

10. All that dancing makes a girl pretty parched. What does she reach for when she needs to quench a burning thirst?

a. orange juice
b. Pepsi
c. Sprite
d. iced tea

11. Even celebrities have their "most embarrassing moments." What onstage blunder would this star probably like to forget ... but can't?

a. when she collided with her dancer T.J.
b. when she ran on stage with her pants unzipped
c. when she forgot the words to "I Will Still Love You"
d. when she slipped on a cupcake someone left on the stage

12. Surprise! Britney has bad habits just like everybody else. What bothersome behavior is she trying to conquer?

a. twirling her hair
b. never cleaning her room
c. chewing with her mouth open
d. biting her nails

13. She may be cute, but Britney's not afraid to break a sweat. Besides dancing up a storm on tour, she likes to swim and take on her brother in a game of one-on-one hoops. She also likes watching basketball on the tube. Which team does she root for?

a. Chicago Bulls
b. Los Angeles Lakers
c. Utah Jazz
d. Miami Heat

14. Before she hit it big in the music world, Britney did some small-screen time in a bunch of TV commercials. Which of these does not appear on her acting resumé?

a. a commercial for barbeque sauce
b. a commercial for a hotel
c. a commercial for toothpaste
d. a commercial for a local phone network

15. Nobody can forget Britney's breakout hit "...Baby One More Time." Funny thing is, the song wasn't originally written for her. She got it after another group's record label passed on it. Which group was the song actually written for?

a. TLC
b. B*Witched
c. Spice Girls
d. Backstreet Boys

16. If you went to Britney's house to hang out, you'd see that her room is full of:

a. posters of *NSYNC
b. a collection of dolls and angels
c. tons of dried flowers
d. postcards she's collected from all over the world

17. The song "Soda Pop" (one of her favorites) is part of the soundtrack for what hit TV show?

a. "Sabrina, the Teenage Witch"
b. "Buffy the Vampire Slayer"
c. "Dawson's Creek"
d. "Felicity"

LEFT TO RIGHT: MARC BAPTISTE/OUTLINE (4), JON RAGEL/OUTLINE

Test your B.I.Q.

Britney Intelligence Quotient!

18. While Britney's jamming away in the "...Baby One More Time" video, there's a guy in the bleachers who's checking her out. Who is he in real life?

a. an ex-boyfriend
b. a good friend she's known since kindergarten
c. just some random guy
d. her cousin

19. Back home, Britney's friends have been known to call her by what nickname?

a. Brit-Brit
b. Tiny
c. Britty
d. Baby

20. When we look at this girl, we can't help thinking she's got incredible style. But even stars have someone they look up to. Who are Britney's favorite fashion icons?

a. Gwyneth Paltrow and Calista Flockhart
b. Jennifer Aniston and Jennifer Love Hewitt
c. Gwen Stefani and Courtney Love
d. Julia Roberts and Niki Taylor

21. With a red-hot singing career and serious talk about her getting her own television show, what's left for the darling diva? Well, how about the fashion world? Which hip design label has used Britney in ad campaigns?

a. Rampage
b. Guess
c. Tommy Hilfiger
d. Abercrombie & Fitch

22. Sugar and spice and everything nice ... Britney's not that much of a cliché, but like lots of girls she likes to get, well, girlie from time to time. And that includes smelling sweet. What's her favorite scent?

a. vanilla
b. juicy berry
c. lavender
d. peaches and cream

23. Britney's the first to admit she's a shopaholic. What's the one thing she simply can't resist buying, even though she's already got tons of them?

a. shoes
b. lipsticks
c. comfy cardigans
d. sunglasses

24. With a December birthday, this babe's a Sagittarius. Sags are what type of sign?

a. earth
b. fire
c. air
d. water

25. And they're known for being:

a. sensitive and moody
b. aggressive, take-charge kind of people
c. outgoing and cheerful
d. dreamy homebodies

26. Britney's debut set a serious record. She became the first female artist to have both a debut single and a debut album simultaneously holding down the No. 1 spots on the Billboard charts. On what day was her album released in U.S. stores?

a. Jan. 1, 1999
b. Feb. 1, 1999
c. Jan. 12, 1999
d. Feb. 14, 1999

27. With all of the traveling she's done, Britney didn't keep the same school schedule most of her friends did. Still, she realized how important education is, and she does plan to go to college someday. When she hits the books, what's her favorite subject?

a. math
b. history
c. art
d. English

28. Like we said, there's nothing this girl likes better than a day of shopping. (It kind of fits that her first tour took her through the malls of America!) Which of these stores is not one of her favorite places to spend a little cash?

a. Contempo Casuals
b. The Gap
c. Bebe
d. A/X

29. If she's in the mood for a good chick flick, which of these is Britney most likely to pop into the VCR?

a. Beauty and the Beast
b. Pretty Woman
c. Ever After
d. Steel Magnolias

30. And something silly and simple to wrap it all up: What's Britney's favorite color?

a. hot pink
b. baby blue
c. bright red
d. pale purple ♥

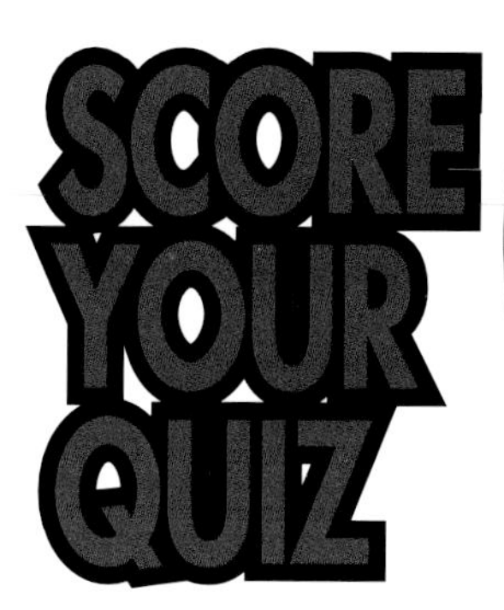

"Test Your B.I.Q." Answers

1. b, 2. c, 3. d, 4. a, 5. c, 6. b, 7. d, 8. a, 9. b, 10. c, 11. d, 12. d, 13. a, 14. c, 15. a, 16. b, 17. a, 18. d, 19. a, 20. b, 21. c, 22. a, 23. d, 24. b, 25. c, 26. c, 27. d, 28. a, 29. d, 30. b

23 to 30 points

So when is your Britney biography going to be published?

You know enough about the talented Ms. Spears to fill a book. Whether it's her favorite movie or the snack she likes to chomp, you've got the answers nailed. Clearly, this star is one of your favorites, and you're always up on the latest Britney trivia, like who she's seeing and when she's performing. If we had to guess, we'd say your room is probably full of books about her, and you've probably been known to wear some of her signature looks.

16 to 22 points

Pick a fact, any fact.

You've been on the Britney bandwagon since day one, and you're pretty well read when it comes to this singing sensation. You've even been known to buy new Britney mags whenever you see them at the newsstand. But no matter how much you like to find out new stuff about her life, you're interested in lots of other things, too. In fact, you've got the best of both worlds: You can have a blast as a fabulous fan and enjoy being a teenage girl without getting lost in Britney mania. But hey, you wouldn't say no to concert tickets ...

9 to 15 points

Sort of Spears savvy

You love her songs and watch her videos. You read about her when you can, but you don't go out of your way to load up on factoids about Britney's life and loves. Frankly, there are too many other things out there vying for your attention. If you ever feel at a loss when your friends start swapping the latest celeb gossip, just change the subject. (If it really gets to you, you can always try reading a few extra articles about the pop princess. That will get you in the know in no time.)

0 to 8 points

Britney who?

You might think you're a Britney scholar, but your score says something else. You obviously have an interest in the diva or you wouldn't have bought this book, but you've got a long way to go before you can consider yourself an expert on her life. Maybe you just started listening to her music, or maybe you just haven't made an effort to get to know the girl behind the songs. You can still have a great time singing along, just don't bet your friends that you know more about Brit-Brit than they do.

LEFT TO RIGHT: MARC BAPTISTE/OUTLINE (3), TIMOTHY WHITE/OUTLINE, MARC ROYCE/OUTLINE

FLASH

Even before hitting it big with "...Baby One

By David Fantle and Tom Johnson

Few entertainers had as good a year as Britney Spears did in 1999.

Her debut CD, "...Baby One More Time," hit No. 1 on the *Billboard* album chart, and it has gone on to sell an astonishing 12 million copies in the United States alone. She staged her first world tour and released several hit singles, including "Sometimes" and "(You Drive Me) Crazy."

BACK!

e Time," Britney was destined to be a star.

FLASHBACK!

destined to be a star

Unlike some male pop artists who have enjoyed success with a mostly female fan base, Britney is proving popular with fans of both genders.

"Guys are into her because she's cute, and girls like her because she's not trying too hard," was how *NSYNC's JC Chasez, a friend of Britney's, described her appeal to *People*.

But ask fans like 17-year-old Jake Zarling, who lives in suburban Milwaukee, and he's even more direct.

"She's hot!" he exclaimed.

Jake has even reserved a coveted place in his bedroom (right above his bed's headboard) for a poster of his favorite star. This is no small accomplishment for Britney, since her poster shares the room with a dresser-top full of athletic trophies, team banners and photos of his all-male sports heroes — Michael Jordan and Green Bay Packers quarterback Brett Favre.

Jake's sentiments are clearly shared by the large contingent of young males who attend Britney's sold-out shows.

While Britney's appeal is highest with teenage fans, her singable, danceable music has also caught on with toddlers, much to the confusion of young parents, most of whom ask, "Britney who?" At a recent dance class of mostly preschool and elementary school girls, the *Honolulu Advertiser* noted that the kids had no interest in moving to the beat of Barney or the Teletubbies. When asked whom they wanted to groove to, they collectively screamed, "Britney Spears! Britney Spears!"

So how did this young superstar get her start?

Southern Belle

Britney Jean Spears was born on Dec. 1, 1981, in the small Louisiana town of Kentwood (population 2,500), about an hourlong drive north of New Orleans. Her father, Jamie, works in the construction trade and her mother, Lynne, is a second-grade schoolteacher. Britney has a 22-year-old brother, Bryan (a sports administration major at Southwest Mississippi Community College), and a 9-year-old sister, Jamie Lynn. A rambunctious toddler, Britney was given the nickname Brit-Brit.

Britney never disses her hometown, although she jokingly told an online chat audience, "It's not very hip at all. You have to travel 30 minutes just to get to McDonald's."

By all accounts, Britney's childhood in Kentwood was normal and included regular church-going (she's a Baptist), a practice she continues today.

"I still try to get to church even when I'm traveling," she said. "But I have my Bible and say my prayers every night."

Kentwood's most famous export took a shine to performing at age 2, when she began singing and dancing for imaginary audiences. At age 5, she sang "What Child Is This?" at her kindergarten graduation.

"She would put on makeup and sing to herself in the bathroom mirror," brother Bryan told *People*.

"I would get on my mom's nerves," added Britney. "When I was a little girl, I was always performing. I remember buying 'Thriller' (Michael Jackson's mega-hit album), and I used to dance around the room all the time. I probably drove my mom mad. She must have thought she had a problem child. But I didn't get into show business because I've got a pushy mother.

***BRITNEY'S SCHOOL DAYS!** From left to right: Britney (left) named "Junior High Beauty" at Parklane Academy in McComb, Miss., in 1997; Britney (second from right) in her Algebra I class; Britney (left) as freshman year homeroom secretary; posing with Mason Statham in 1996 "Junior High Most Beautiful" photo; Britney (left, No. 25) on the junior varsity basketball team; Britney's "Junior High Who's Who" photo in 1997; young Britney named 7th grade "Class Favorite"; Britney as freshman maid in the 1997 Homecoming Court.*

She's not one of those stage moms. It was always me who wanted to do all of the performing."

Added Britney to CNN: "I was actually really obnoxious. I was always singing to the radio and always dancing and doing my own thing. My mother took me to a dance instructor. All she did was teach dance, but she told my mother, 'Your daughter can sing. Why don't you start entering her in singing and dancing contests?' One thing led to another and things my mom thought were really obnoxious turned out to be really cool."

While mimicking the Whitney Houston and Mariah Carey hits she listened to constantly, Britney developed her distinctive singing style.

As a child, Britney told *Twist*, "I had moods where I just wanted to get on the go-cart – that's not a girlie thing to do. But then I'd have moments where I'd go into my playhouse and play dolls for six hours."

At age 8, to supplement her dancing lessons, Britney took up gymnastics and briefly attended Bela Karolyi's training camp.

Meeting 'The Mouse'

At age 9, Britney learned that The Disney Channel was holding auditions in Atlanta for its revival of the '50s *Mickey Mouse Club*. While she made a positive impression on the producers, Britney was deemed too young and received her walking papers. It was to be a rare taste of rejection for the up-and-coming star. Nevertheless, an astute producer still helped Britney, who was simply too young for the Disney show, secure an agent.

Undaunted, and now with her parents' full support, Britney, her mom and little sister Jamie Lynn moved to New York City's rugged Hell's Kitchen neighborhood to help nurture Britney's artistic talents. For the next three summers, Britney honed her skills at the prestigious Off-Broadway Dance Center and the Professional Performing Arts School. She also began landing spots for national TV commercials and Off-Broadway shows, including the 1991 comedy, *Ruthless*, based on the 1956 thriller *The Bad Seed*.

"At 10, I was playing this really bad child who seems real sweet... but she's evil, too," said Britney. "It was so much fun." The 10-year-old Britney was also a *Star Search* winner.

Britney took the move to New York in stride.

"I was really thankful because you know most parents push the child," she said. "I was the one who was pushing. I'm from a small town and people were like, 'You're sending your daughter to New York? Are you crazy?' But I was the one who wanted to do it and I'm thankful because they were so supportive.

"I really didn't like (New York City) at first," she added. "And my mom was like, 'Baby, whenever you want to go home, we'll go.' "

At age 11, she now had the maturity and credentials to audition again for *The New Mickey Mouse Club*, although she remained the show's youngest performer. She landed a coveted spot and for the next two years had mouse ears almost permanently attached to her head.

"(Being a Mouseketeer) was a lot of fun because I

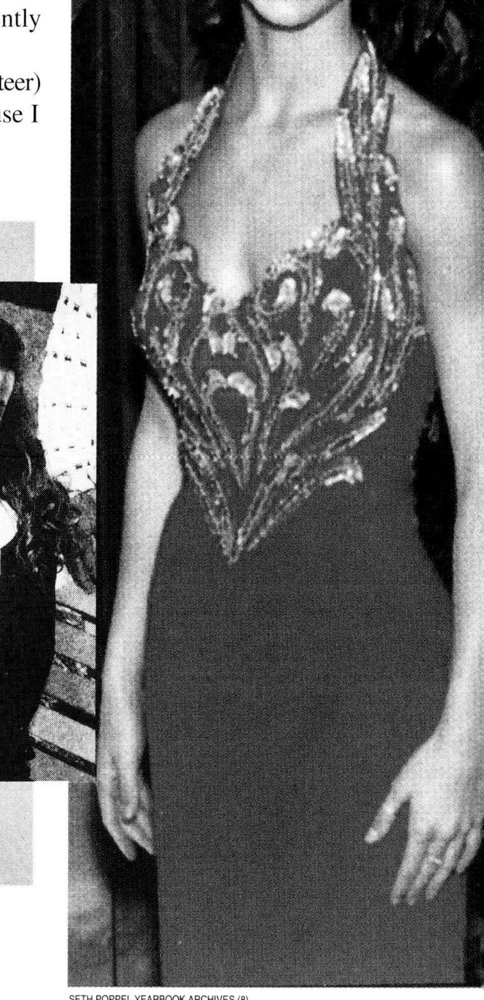

SETH POPPEL YEARBOOK ARCHIVES (8)

was like a baby," she told an online chat audience. "I was 11 or 12 and was the youngest one on the show, so people catered to me. Just being in Disney World alone was a lot of fun. There were about 20 kids with me; I just loved it there. It's still my favorite place to go, just like everyone else. I mean, it's Disney World for heaven's sake!"

Making Music

While performing for *The New Mickey Mouse Club*, Britney realized she wanted to pursue a career in music. Britney's class of fellow Mouseketeers also included future stars Keri Russell of TV's *Felicity* and JC Chasez and Justin Timberlake of *NSYNC.

After performing on the show for two years, Britney, now 14, handed in her mouse ears and returned to Kentwood for one normal year at high school. She actually attended a private high school, Park Lane Academy in nearby McComb, Miss. But Britney, who now had a taste of stardom, felt stifled by the school's strict rules. She compared her situation to the opening scene in the movie *Clueless* – with all the cliques, from the cheerleaders and jocks, to the burnouts.

Britney's mom, Lynne, told *People*, "Going into the middle of the year, she was antsy."

Added Britney: "I did the homecoming and the prom thing, and I was totally bored. ... I started getting itchy to get out again and see the world. I need to sing, and I love to travel."

The aforementioned prom date was with a young man name Reg, whom Britney says was her only real boyfriend until recently The two were together for two years before Britney's budding career and frequent road trips put the relationship on ice.

"It wasn't that I was changing," Britney said of the breakup "We broke up before any of my success had happened. He becam insecure about himself, I felt. I wasn't gonna do anything. I'm straight-up, honest person, and if I was gonna do anything, I'd tel him before I'd do it and end the relationship. I was really hea over heels in love. I don't think I'll ever love somebody like tha again. I just woke up one day, and click, it was gone."

Britney maintained her studies by enrolling in a Universit of Nebraska home schooling program. "I worry about he terribly," Lynne said. "But I'm so much happier knowing she' doing what she really wants to do."

Rolling Stone describes her ranch-style home this way "Britney's 'girly' bedroom, like the rest of her house, is awash i floral patterns and frills."

Now a seasoned performer, an audition for an all-girl voca group led to her developing a solo career as a pop singer as we as continuing her high school studies with tutors.

"I need a lot of help in geometry and Spanish," she said. " know I've had to give up stuff to do this, but I don't miss hig school. When I was home, every weekend we'd go out and do th same thing. It's wonderful as long as you love what you're doing but I'd rather be doing this!"

When Britney turned 15, Lynne sent a homemade demo tap of her daughter to Larry Rudolph, a well-connected New Yor City entertainment lawyer. He became her co-manager and soo signed Britney to a recording contract with Jive Records.

After auditioning for a Jive executive by singing "Jesu Loves Me" and Whitney Houston's "I Have Nothing," Jiv

BRITNEY SPEARS THROUGH THE YEARS! From left to right: Britney's 1st grade photo in 1989; her 2nd grade photo in 1990; her 3rd grade photo in 1991; Britney's 6th grade photo in 1994; Britney named "Junior High Beauty" in 7th grade in 1995; Britney in her 8th grade photo in 1996; her freshman year class photo in 1997; Britney looks all grown up in 1998.

Records chief Barry Weiss signed the 15-year-old and shipped her off to Sweden to craft her debut album with writer/producer Max Martin, the man with the golden touch behind the music of Backstreet Boys.

Food Court Queen

Superstardom did not come overnight. With no recording to promote, Britney did what other pop stars, such as Debbie Gibson and Tiffany, did before her: She headlined at shopping malls throughout the country. Unsuspecting parents taking their teenage kids to the Gap and Old Navy were suddenly curious onlookers, diverted to an attractive young teenager belting out pop tunes in the middle of the mall. As the mall tour grew, so did the size of her audience. It wasn't long before poor Britney was being mauled by fans at malls nationwide.

It was a dicey career move, especially considering that the careers of Gibson and Tiffany quickly crashed, but Britney didn't seem to care.

"It was crazy," she told *People*. "No one knew who I was, but I could see that they really enjoyed the music. And I got a lot of shopping done!"

The Big Break

Little did Britney know what was in store for her when in 1998, she went into the recording studio to lay down the tracks for her debut album, "...Baby One More Time."

The next chapter of her life was about to begin, and there would be no looking back. ♥

SETH POPPEL YEARBOOK ARCHIVES (7)

BRIT

NEY LIVE

Miss Spears gives her fans a night to remember

By Seth Gardner

LEFT: MIKE KLINE/WILDSHOTS LLC

On a balmy Friday evening in suburban Chicago, thousands of young people are lined up outside an enormous amphitheater, chatting excitedly about what the night will bring.

"I can't wait to hear what song she sings first," one girl says. "I hope it's "... Baby One More Time" because that's my favorite!"

"I love how she dances," another girl chimes in. "And her dancers are the best!"

A teenage boy with a huge "I ♥ Britney" sign adds, "I hear she wears a lot of different costumes. I hope she wears that red thing from the "Oops! ... I Did It Again" video. That was so cool!"

The "she" the youngsters are referring to is, of course, Britney Spears, who comes to Chicago on her summer-long "Oops! ... I Did It Again" concert tour. It's just one show among many she has scheduled throughout the United States, but Britney knows that every concert is important. For the kids in her audience, that one show is the most important thing to happen in their lives since ... well, since the last Britney concert they attended. And Britney is more than ready to put on a spectacular show for everyone.

"My fans are all I care about," Britney says. "As long as they are happy, that's all that matters."

When the New World Music Theater gates open promptly at 6 p.m., throngs of kids and their families run toward the huge lawn area, where the seats are "first come, first served." For those fortunate enough to have a reserved seat closer to Britney's huge stage, it's time to relax, grab a soda and take a look at the merchandise Britney has for sale. From cute T-shirts and posters to teddy bears and brightly lit glowsticks, there's a little something for everybody. There's even a booth sponsored by "Got Milk?" where fans can get their photo taken with a life-size cardboard cutout of Britney. It's almost as good as meeting the real Britney!

There isn't much time to waste, though, because by 7:15 p.m. the first of three opening acts is ready to warm up the huge crowd. The cheers are deafening as popular foursome No Authority take the stage. The boys – Ricky G, Eric Stretch, Tommy McCarthy and Danny Zavatsky – get fans danci

"Oops! ... I Did It Again" Tour Song List

1. (You Drive Me) Crazy
2. Stronger
3. What U See (Is What U Get)
4. From The Bottom Of My Broken Heart
5. Born To Make You Happy
6. Lucky
7. Sometimes
8. Don't Let Me Be The Last To Know
9. And The Beat Goes On
10. Don't Go Knockin' On My Door
11. (I Can't Get No) Satisfaction

ENCORE

12. ... Baby One More Time
13. Oops! ... I Did It Again

ith the infectious "What I Wanna Do," song many had probably heard before Radio Disney. After an excellent per-rmance of "I'm Telling You This" from Authority's new CD, the group pulls t folding chairs and does some phat nce moves to the guys' new single, an I Get Your Number." Very fun!

Next up is the all-girl group iosense, and Jenny, Nikki, Veronica, nay and Mandy keep the crowd mped up with their high-energy ging and awesome dance moves. ys and girls alike are all smiles as osense performs "Go Baby Go" and group's first single, "Say No More." This group has a lot of talent, so don't be surprised if these girls make it big!

About 8:20 p.m., the three members of BBMak – Mark Barry, Christian Burns and Ste McNally – bring their guitars front and center for an exciting performance of songs from their first CD, "Sooner or Later." These guys may not do any synchronized dances, but the fans obviously love them for their musical talents. Mark, Christian and Ste write and perform their own songs, and their beautiful harmonies are mesmerizing. From the crowd pleasing sounds of "Unpredictable" to the Top 20 smash "Back Here," it's clear that BBMak has a bright future!

BRITNEY

Now comes the moment each fan is waiting for. As the lights dim and the sun sets behind the now-full lawn area, two large video screens on the left and right sides of the stage come to life. No, it's not Britney yet, but it is her commercial for Clairol Herbal Essences shampoo, one of the sponsors of Britney's "Oops! ... I Did It Again" tour! The commercial shows scenes from all of Britney's music videos, and each quick glimpse provokes a collective scream from all the fans.

MIKE KLINE/WILDSHOTS LLC (2); RIGHT: BILL APTER (3)

"FINALLY, AT 9:10 P.M., THE LIGHTS GO OFF, AND THE HUGE, BLACK 'GOT MILK?' CURTAIN DROPS TO THE STAGE."

The fans are teased even more as Britney's commercial for "Got Milk?" airs next. When will she start the show?!

Finally, at 9:10 p.m., the lights go off, and the huge, black "Got Milk?" curtain drops to the stage. The wait is over! The video screen behind the stage lights up with three faces that look like Britney Spears from outer space. "You have just accessed The Britney Spears Experience," the Britney faces inform the crowd. "Come with me ... let's go!"

Then some loud fireworks go off as a large, silver orb resembling a big Christmas tree ornament descends from catwalks above the stage. The silver sphere continues its slow drop in front of a star-lit black backdrop and a curtain covered with what look like oversized diamonds. Shrieking in anticipation, Britney's fans know what has to come next, and they are not disappointed. Britney emerges from the ball whi[le] Britney's eight dancers – six boys an[d] two girls – form a tight circle around her. They stop and hold still momentar[i]ly, then launch into an amazing dance routine as the five-piece band plays "(You Drive Me) Crazy" from Britney's first CD. Wearing a flashy silver half-jacket over a hot pink halter top, Britney has a beaming smile on her face as she yells for the crowd to sing along with the chorus. What an incredible opening!

Not wanting the energy to drop even for a second, Britney finishes "(You Drive Me) Crazy" and goes imm[e]diately into "Stronger," a fantastic up-tempo song from Britney's new CD. T[he] dance moves on this song are AMAZING! At one point, Britney stands in front of a curtain that's cut in strips li[ke] the curtains you see in automatic car washes. As Britney sings the final ch[o]rus, the dancers' come through the

MIKE KLINE/WILDSHOTS LLC (4); BILL APT

curtain and wave in undulating motions all around Britney. What a unique sight!

All of the Chicago fans are still standing and screaming as Britney starts her third song, "What U See (Is What U Get)." Britney is still wearing the pink halter top and shiny silver pants, but now she's got a big, pink cowboy hat to go with it. Britney's dancers have colorful cowboy hats, too, that match their brightly colored shirts. While Britney sings and clutches a silver pole atop a pyramid-shaped platform, the dancers surprise fans by pushing the platform across the stage, using circular dancing motions to stay in sync while moving the platform from the right side of the stage to the left. What a neat idea!

B R I T N E Y

By this point, the fans are out of breath from all the excitement, so you can imagine how Britney and her dancers must feel! It's obviously time to slow things down a little, so Britney casually takes a seat in a black, high-back chair and sings her hit ballad, "From The Bottom Of My Broken Heart." As Britney sings and her dancers take a breather on the tall steps behind her, all the fans from the front row to the back end of the lawn wave their Britney glowsticks from side to side. Meanwhile, the video screen behind Britney shows some clips from the "Broken Heart" music video, then cuts to a great live close-up of her smiling. She's obviously having a great

time performing tonight!

As Britney's band finishes the song, the superstar singer quickly runs off the stage and her two wonderful backup singers step forward. Behind them, the video screen lights up with five well-known faces – yep, it's *NSYNC! It seems it's time for a "What Would You Do To Meet Britney?" contest, and the members of *NSYNC are going to ask four preselected fans to perform a few tricks. The catch? The person the fans cheer the loudest for will get to stay on stage and meet Britney! How cool!

Chris Kirkpatrick gives Mission On to the first contestant: "Bark like a dog!" The girl barks very loudly and gets a lot of applause and laughing from the crowd. Mission Two comes from JC Chasez: "Flop like a fish out o water!" The boy quickly gets on his stomach and does his best fish imitation, getting even more laughs from th fans. This is one tough contest!

Justin Timberlake informs the nex girl about Mission Three: "Sing your favorite Britney song!" The contestant looks a little nervous, but she does a pretty nice job singing the chorus to " Baby One More Time." What can top that? Well, Lance Bass is ready with Mission Four: "Walk like a chicken!"

MIKE KLINE/WILDSHOTS LLC (6); INSET: BILL APTE

The boy who is the fourth and final contestant wastes no time, strutting across the stage, flapping his arms and clucking like the craziest chicken on earth!

Now it's time for the audience's vote, and it's not even close. Bryce, the best chicken-walker in Chicago, gets to meet his idol! Before going into her next song, Britney comes out and gives Bryce a huge hug before her backup singers take a quick Polaroid photo and escort the boy off the stage. What a great moment for him!

B R I T N E Y

Now it's time for Britney's fifth song, "Born To Make You Happy," and the stage has a totally different look. Britney – wearing a cute white shirt with a kitten's face on the front, along with white pants and simple sneakers – sits on a large bed surrounded by a set designed to look like we might actually be in Britney's bedroom down in Kentwood, Louisiana. There are book shelves, a desk and a bureau with lots of mirrors – essential for any girl who has to put on make-up before heading off to school! Britney sits and sings from the bed during most of the song, then stopping to pick up a framed photo off an adjacent nightstand and gaze at it while she sings. I wonder whose photo was in that frame?

Meanwhile, Britney's awesome dancers do some solo moves behind her, gradually gathering together as the songs nears its end. Then, the music suddenly switches to a conga-style tune, and the dancers surround Britney for a few Gloria Estefan-inspired moves.

BRITNEY LIVE

MIKE KLINE/WILDSHOTS LLC

Britney's next song is her new single, "Lucky," and the choreography simply shows Britney singing in her room, looking a little sad, while her backup singers try to console her. It's a neat setup, especially when the dancers rejoin the group wearing sailor outfits. Just like in the music video for "Lucky," Britney sings into old-time microphones while the "sailors" dance around her. Even though her youngest fans may not realize that Britney is trying to imitate glamorous stars from decades ago, the parents in the audience are pretty impressed with the unique approach to the song.

Now, it's time to have a little fun again. Britney's "bedroom" has a big door on the far side, and now all the dancers are on the other side of it, pounding on the door and yelling, "Wake up Britney!" Britney eventually gets up from her bed and comes across to open the door. Once she opens it, the familiar sounds of "Sometimes" come from the band. With the fans singing every word of the song and the video screen showing clips from the popular "Sometimes" video, Britney and her dancers have a great time goofing off. They play with stuffed animals, throw around beach balls and even attack each other with squirt guns! The revelry concludes with a huge pillow fight and feathers flying around everywhere as the song ends. So, who's gonna clean up that mess?!

After a minute or so, the lights on the stage come back on, and the fans see Britney sitting atop the huge steps in the middle, looking very glamorous in a white dress with a train that goes all the way down the steps. She takes moment to thank the fans for coming, reminding every one of them that the are the ones "making her dreams cor true." Britney then says she's going tc perform her favorite song on her new CD, "Don't Let Me Be The Last To Know." This song is a special treat fo fans who saw Britney perform in Chicago a few months earlier. During that show, Britney did a "sneak preview" of only two songs from her the unreleased new CD, and this stunnin ballad was one of them. If anyone ev says Britney doesn't have a good voi just make them listen to this song. It' one of her best!

After each member of Britney's band takes a brief opportunity to perform a solo (including her drummer, "DJ Slam"), the young superstar and her posse of dancers return to perfo a groovy, reggae-influenced version Sonny and Cher's 1967 hit, "And The

MIKE KLINE/WILDSHOTS LLC (3); BILL AP

eat Goes On." Britney's unique, imono-style outfit is complemented y the dancers' classy black-and-white uits and top hats. Fans look up in mazement as Britney ends the song uspended by wires about 20 feet bove the stage, her legs covered by a d, white and blue cloak that sort of oks like an American flag.

The cloak then comes off to reveal itney's new outfit, a cool lavender mpsuit. The dancers have changed, o, into baggy black pants and glimery red vests. Accompanied by a nky video in the background, the ncers get in a pyramid like cheeraders would and do synchronized oves to "Don't Go Knockin' On y Door."

Next up is a classic: Britney's renion of the Rolling Stones' classic them, "(I Can't Get No) Satisfaction." me critics say Britney should never ve recorded this song, but in concert e shines, rolling through the song ile perched in a throne fit for a

"THE VIDEO SCREEN TURNS ON AND TELLS FANS TO 'MAKE SOME NOISE!'"

queen. Her dancers, dressed all in black, stand all around Britney and fan her with huge, multicolored feathers. As the song ends, Britney's throne slides back into the stage (what a cool effect!), and the entire amphitheater goes dark except for the soft, green lights from thousands of glowsticks.

B R I T N E Y

It seems like the show is over, but the fans know it can't be. It's only just after 10 p.m., and how could Britney

not sing her two biggest hits? That's what everyone came to see and hear!

After what seemed like an eternity (but it was probably only a minute or so!), the video screen turns on and tells fans to "Make Some Noise!" Then the lights go on to reveal a stage set up to look like a high school classroom. A row of school desks lines the front of the stage, and lockers stand behind them adorned with graffiti like "I ♥ Bob" and "Kid Rock Rules." Pretty funny!

Sitting in the center desk is Britney, but it looks like she's asleep! Of course, she's not! The "school bell" rings, and Britney's ready to go! She starts "... Baby One More Time" wearing an outfit much like the one she had in the music video: red plaid skirt, white dress shirt, black knee-high socks. The male dancers are wearing traditional blue dress shirts and khaki pants.

Then, suddenly, in the middle of the song, everyone rips off their costumes to reveal fun outfits right out of Abercrombie & Fitch! As confetti cannons go off, fans see Britney sporting a midriff-baring red football jersey (with the number 10!) and a cool khaki skirt. The dancers and backup singers get into the act, too, showing as much "school spirit" as possible!

The stage goes dark again, however, and everyone knows what's next. It's time for the 13th and final song of the night, the one that has made Britney's new CD such a huge success: "Oops! ... I Did It Again." Before it starts, though, the space-age Britney Spears faces return to the video screen. "You have just seen The Britney Spears Experience," the faces tell the anxious crowd. "I hope you enjoyed the journey."

The fans respond with enthusiastic screams as Britney and her dancers return. Britney's wearing a black, two-piece jumpsuit imprinted with orange flames, and her dancers are wearing orange, construction-worker-style outfits. They perform "Oops!" wildly while huge windsocks in the shape of flames blow up from the stage. Britney wraps up the final chorus atop a platform tha rises about 20 feet over the stage whil the "Oops!" music video ends on the screen. What a thrilling finish!

B R I T N E Y

As the lights come on, youngsters throughout the audience realize the show is truly over. They grab their T-shirts, glowsticks and posters and hea to the parking lot, still amazed at wha they had just witnessed.

Britney says her fans' happiness i her only concern, and if she could hea her fans' comments after the Chicago show, she would certainly be thrilled.

One girl, her eyes aglow, says to her mother: "That was the best ever. Can we come back tomorrow?"

Maybe not tomorrow, but next time. B

MIKE KLINE/WILDSHOTS LL

BRITNEY
LIVE

britney live

Rosemont, Illinois • Allstate Arena • March 22-23, 2000

BRITNEY PHOTO BY SPORTS IMAGERY

britney live

Tampa, Florida • Ice Palace • March 31, 2000

We ♥ U
Britney
Rules!
BRITNEY~
Baby!
#1
World
Britney

britney live

Miami, Florida • American Airlines Arena • April 1, 2000

BRITNE
WiLL you
MARRY ME
BRITNEY
U-DRIVE
ME CRAZY
Arena
Americ
UFO
BRITNEY

britney live

Daytona Beach, Florida • Ocean Center • April 2, 2000

FAN PHOTOS BY STACEY HEWEY
BRITNEY PHOTO BY SPORTS IMAGERY